Tank Tales-A Nursing Home Visit

A Children's Guide to Nursing Homes and Dementia.

TANK SHICK

Archway Publishing books may be ordered through booksellers or by contacting:

Archway Publishing
1663 Liberty Drive
Bloomington, IN 47403
www.archwaypublishing.com
1 (888) 242-5904

Interior Art Credit: Thomas McCormick

ISBN: 978-1-4808-6829-8 (sc)
ISBN: 978-1-4808-6828-1 (e)

Print information available on the last page.

Archway Publishing rev. date: 4/26/2019

Tank Tales—A Nursing Home Visit

Hi! My name is Tank and I am a Therapy Dog at a nursing home. My job is to see patients, family, and staff and help them feel better. I love helping people at work. But today things are different. I am seeing my Grandpa for the first time in the nursing home.

Momma and I are going to see Grampa at a nursing home! He has had problems with remembering words and walking, so he lives there now. I have been very sad, but Momma said, "It will make Grandpa feel better." I am excited, but scared. I do not know what it will be like.

My first stop is at the front desk so I can check in and get a treat. Everyone loves petting and talking to me. Of course, I love my new friends. There are many workers at the nursing home. Doctors, nurses, activities people, and cooks in the kitchen. The custodians keep everything clean!

As we walked down the hall, I saw a huge room that looked like a gym. People were learning to walk and practice things they will need to be able to do. They lift weights, ride a big bicycle, and play with lots of different balls. This room is for Physical Therapy. Physical Therapy helps people get stronger, walk or use their hands again, especially after a operation. I like my friends from Physical Therapy. I let people pet me between exercises which makes them smile.

I stop in each room to get pats on my back. People tell me how cute I am and how they love my visits. Nurses, family, and other patients always tell me how handsome I am.

Everyone loves to shake my paw! I have a great job at the nursing home and love getting petted and helping people feel better. What a great job!

I knew Grandpa was in the last room. My tail started wagging fast as we got closer! Grandpa and I were best friends at home. We finally got to Grandpa's room at the end of the hall. I jumped in bed, just like I used to at home!

I have missed giving Grandpa kisses and love, but understand he needs the different kinds of help you get in a nursing home. Sometimes he understands, other times he may not, but it is my job to show you how to help people with memory problems. There are many ways to help!

Having Therapy Dogs like me visit helps many people feel better. I love my job helping people understand what happens in nursing homes. Sometimes people with memory problems can get very confused and it can be scary, but its OK! I know different ways help Grandpa in a nursing home. First, tell him who you are, use his name and look at him when you talk.

Using your body's language, such as smiling, helps Grandpa. During our visits, I ALWAYS sit by Grandpa's side next to his wheel chair. He talks about what we used to do and brings up the good times we had together years ago. It helps Grandpa remember old times with love, happiness, and dogs!

Take things slow and easy, which can get hard some days. BUT, I am known to take it too easy, sometimes falling asleep during visits while I am getting petted.

Seeing people with memory problems can be hard, but I know what to do! I always feel good after visiting the nursing home and helping the people feel better.

Printed in the United States
By Bookmasters